FEEL ALL YOUR FEELINGS: EMOTIONAL POWER FOR GIRLS

By ANNE SWARTZ
A GUIDE

This book is dedicated to Jay Lose, Charles Lose
and
Shana Doyle, Monika Lammers,
Petra Richterová, and Kira Simring for their suggestions.

Copyright © 2023
Text by Anne Swartz

All Rights Reserved. No part of this book may be reproduced or used in any manner without written permission of the copyright owner except for the use of quotations in a book review.

ISBN: 979-8-9876520-8-4 (Paperback)
ISBN: 979-8-9876520-9-1 (eBook)
Published by Aram Samsam Printing

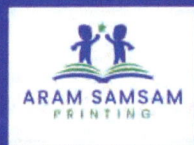

Author's Note

This text references American psychotherapist Gloria Willcox's 1982 Feeling Wheel. Her article and feeling wheel are available at Gloria Willcox, "The Feeling Wheel A Tool for Expanding Awareness of Emotions and Increasing Spontaneity and Intimacy," <u>Transactional Analysis Journal</u>, 12(4) (1982): 274-276.
https://journals.sagepub.com/doi/epdf/10.1177/036215378201200411

This text does not include all feelings she had listed on her wheel, but it does include her color coding: powerful=green, sad=purple, scared=orange, joyful=yellow, mad=red, peaceful=blue

Additionally, this text contains information to help readers be better-informed healthcare consumers. This information reflects my experience and should not be considered medical advice or mental health consultation. Please seek advice from your healthcare professionals.

EXPERIENCE YOUR FEELINGS

We feel less alone when we talk about our feelings. Connecting with others and expressing emotions can be easy one day and hard the next.

This book examines excellent feelings that people embrace and negative ones that some try to ignore. There are also some star pages with questions about your emotions where you can add your ideas.

You may have had different experiences with these feelings or call them other names. Please add the words you use for these feelings on the next page.

Your Names for Feelings

Do you talk about your feelings? Is it easy or difficult for you to understand what you feel?

Feeling confident can be an outcome of feeling good. When we believe in ourselves, we feel glad.

These girls look depressed. A depressing moment can occur, but long-term feelings may require treatment.

A person feeling overloaded may experience fear and doubt. These emotions can feel harsh.

Thoughtfulness means being mindful and understanding of oneself and the needs of others, believing everyone is valuable.

A person feeling angry may also feel bitter, frustrated, or mad. These are all ways of feeling angry.

Satisfaction is a state of pleasure and wonder. It is how you feel when you are happy.

What do you feel now?

These girls feel excited. They feel jolly and animated about their lives, which shows on their happy faces.

These girls all look bored or tired. They have low energy and do not look interested in anything.

These girls are puzzled, confused, or frightened. They may react suddenly or timidly, or uneasily.

The expressions here show feelings of delight and optimism. These people are all bubbly in some way.

A person feeling rage or hate may seem intense because they are upset. They may shout or throw things.

These girls feel secure. They project ease in their surroundings. They are comfortable.

What was it like for you when you had one of these feelings?

These girls feel proud. They each feel glad, which makes them want to express their pleasure.

Shame can make someone feel guilty, ashamed, and sorry. It can even make you want to isolate yourself.

Disappointment or rejection can be painful. If we feel denied of something we want, we may feel discouraged.

These girls are excited. They feel empowered and full of ideas and cheer. They show joy on their faces.

Hurt can be outside or inside our bodies. If we feel upset, we might say, "I am hurt," or "my feelings are hurt."

These girls feel serene, relaxed, and calm. Their faces express good feelings.

Negative feelings can seem intense. They can make it feel like doing anything else is tricky. Have you ever felt like that?

These girls express themselves creatively. They show imagination by moving and making things.

You may feel miserable and lonely. These are common ways of expressing distress.

Feeling limited or less can seem like you need to be noticed. It may feel intense or could feel temporary.

When people feel playful, they are hopeful and carefree, enjoy new things, and are in a good mood.

The feelings here are disgust or revulsion. Their faces show that they say, "Yuck!" or "Gross!"

Trusting in yourself means you believe in yourself. You feel powerful when you trust yourself and your abilities.

Have you watched or noticed someone else when you feel bad? Did they react the same way you do to that feeling?

A successful girl may feel good about what she decides and does. She is happy about her life.

You may feel bored and sleepy when you are tired. You may not want to focus or pay attention then.

Rejection, insecurity, envy, and jealousy can stem from feelings of anger.

These girls are cheerful and happy. They are having fun, which encourages others to feel the same.

These girls feel awkward and look worried and uncomfortable. They also look like they feel unhappy.

When someone feels nurturing, they want to help, care for, protect, and support others.

Sometimes we do not feel like smiling because other things are happening. How does your body show what you think and feel in those moments?

Someone feels valued when they feel seen. These girls all look like they feel valued.

Feeling moody, stressed, or sullen may mean you have a lot going on in your life. It can feel confusing.

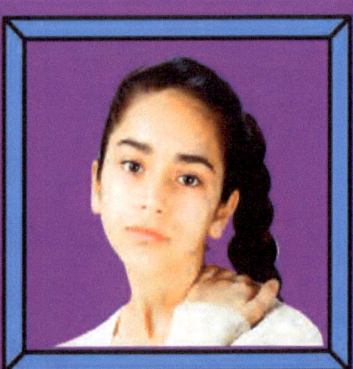

An anxious person feels worried, edgy, or uptight. They may feel uneasy, sometimes for no reason.

Someone feels daring when they take risks and pursue their goals. It may not be easy to do so.

When someone feels hostile, they get nasty toward others. They may also get mean.

A responsive girl is engaged and actively listens to others while considering their needs.

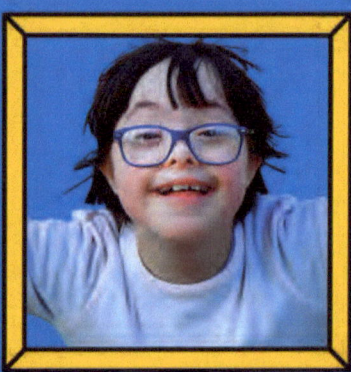

Girls are told to smile more. Boys get told to act tough. Neither is fair. What can we do about it?

When someone thinks smartly and attentively, they try to understand others and be aware.

When someone feels inferior, they experience feelings of unease. They may feel less deserving or less capable.

Fearfulness may make you feel fragile, weak, or anxious, which can feel complicated and confusing.

A joyful and creative person can feel free and inspired as they explore new ideas to express themselves.

When someone feels criticized, they may become picky and frustrated. It can feel awful.

Feeling peaceful and thankful leads to happiness and gratitude for one moment or many moments.

Why do feelings seem busy and difficult sometimes, then quiet and still at other times?

Cheery people are motivated and strong, often feeling important in their life.

Sadness can make you tired or want to cry. You may also feel lonely when you are sad.

When a girl feels like no one sees them or they feel scared, they may feel small and want to withdraw.

Feeling amused and joyful brings happiness and lightness, with excitement and vitality.

If someone feels unsure and mad, they may mistrust others, fueling confusing feelings.

Peacefulness brings serenity, and relaxation to the mind and body, promoting calm and balance.

Which feelings do you enjoy the most? Which emotions make you feel most like yourself?

**How would you complete this sentence?
I feel most powerful when_____.**

www.ingramcontent.com/pod-product-compliance
Lightning Source LLC
Chambersburg PA
CBHW041750040426
42446CB00001B/2